RAEDORAH C. STEWART

[EROTIC] POETRY-TO-READ-ALOUD

Grapes, Watermelon, & Women

Dedication

to all the women/womyn/wommin
femmewomen/MOCwomen
I have longed for, laid with, or laid eyes on
I have listened to, lamented with, and learned from

Acknowledgements

Myself.
I am proud of myself to be healed enough to finally publish
poetry as a collection that I have written, performed,
and laid out in book form since 1980. It's 2024.

I am less afraid. And, if I die before I wake,
I want grown-ass women to read these poems aloud,
to finger ourselves or someone else's glove box,
and not wait 44 years to transcribe their lives in words.

My daughter (née son).
Her poetry and audacity to live keep me living.
Less afraid.

Contents

Preface

"Grapes, Watermelon, and Women" is selected erotic poetry from my terminal anthology, Colored Womyn's Commentary–over 20 years of writing a lot of poetry, performing quite a bit of poetry, and publishing very little poetry.

I write poetry to keep myself company. To talk to whomever listens about real pain and anticipated pleasure. To think through my next move. To work out a bad mistake. To cry when tears won't fall. To laugh at every opportunity. To lament and groan. To celebrate and remember. To leave a legacy of words to my son/sons/daughters, especially the ones I didn't birth but who still need to know.

I perform poetry to tell my colored woman's story. To make the record. To set the record straight. To give voice, loud and clear, to those who'd rather I keep silent.

I learned to love/listen to/make my own colored womyn's commentary by eavesdropping when grown women gathered at the kitchen table instead of playing outside with the rest of the children; by reading grown women's words before I got grown/gone from my mama's house; by daring to live/love like a grown colored woman who expects to live forever despite efforts to kill me/spirit/mind.
Some of the words are autobiographical, indeed. Still, most are what Audre Lorde would name biomythological: my voice/lens for recording what happens to/around me. True and valid and necessary.

"Grapes, Watermelon, & Women" is a whole-body experience meant to be read aloud, cried over, laughed about, danced to, and shared as pillow talk and poetry slams.

Be sure to get my permission to publish or record for performance. Better still, invite me to read/perform/compose for your next colored womyn's gathering.
Raedorah Con'ett

Daylight

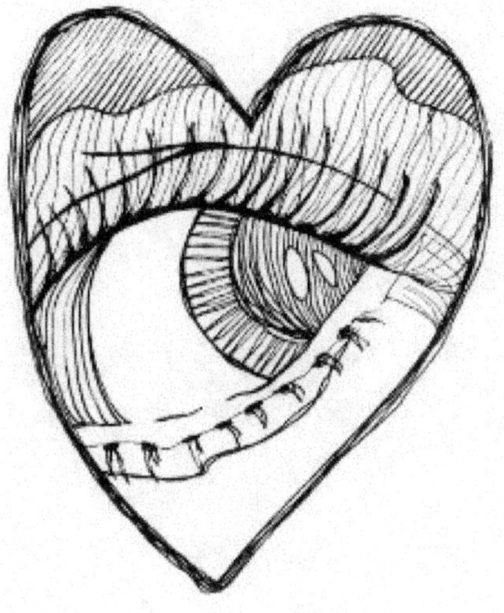

Cooking Like a Colored Woman, 1996

(Madeline)

She was cooking like a colored woman
and she didn't even need a pot
wearing a tight black suit
against the summertime's hot

She was wearing a wide-brimmed hat
hiding alla her face except one eye
stepping out in high-heeled pumps
with a matching bag against her thigh

She was cooking
the men were on simmer
the women were on boil
and the switch in her hips
was very well-oiled.

Like a colored woman
adding flava to the room
leaving perfume in her wake
past rolling eyes and watering mouths
doing the damage of a major earthquake.

She was cooking like a colored woman.

Tacky Women, 1995

Tacky women
invade your roots by hand
to see if you are weaved

Tacky women
tell you this week when it doesn't matter
that your slip was hanging last month

Tacky women
asks if your "bling-bling" are real diamonds
all the while implying that they are not

Tacky women
tell your good news before you can
and your bad news in mixed company.

Hey sister,
when you look in the mirror,
does a tacky woman look back?

To Tell the Truth, 2002

to tell the truth
sometimes, I just don't get it

like
when your poetry mixes metaphor
like
when your prayers mix gods
like
when your passion mixes peoples

don't mind me none but
sometimes, I just don't get it

Hope for Summertime, 1980
(Hope)

I heard Hope singing
"Summertime"
making it sound like summertime.

Vengeful heat spewed forth
from a rasped voice
But cooled down, cooled down
cooled by that mellow noted lemonade
Easy living
Living is easy.

Catching the summertime breeze
Dusty film of memories made
110° in the shade
As Hope sang "Summertime"

"Summertime" in 2-4 time
Making me feel like this summer's mine!

commentary on emilie, 2000

Feasting on your words
I eat my fill to wholeness
       body healing
       mind nourishing
       spirit-stirring
Satisfied.
Waiting for your next invitation
I take note of where I've
       given over
       grown up
       came out
Inspired.
Fingering your new, next book
I inhale (deeply) fragrant hope of
       increasing voice
       making sense
       becoming, still
Refined.
But now   In your presence
       I am speechless.

Commentary on Julianne, 2000

First thought
      you wear red – well
'til you opened your mouth
and molten lava spewed forth
erupting from a belly
soul-fed on grit-truth and raw-reality

'til you wrote your words
and reader notes red-lined
emphases and epiphanies
confirming knowledge and catalyzing change

'til you came and stood beside me
      couldn't hear what you said
      couldn't comprehend what you wrote
for trying to figure out whether I was being
      warmed or burned
      refined or consumed
      empowered or destroyed

'cause fire is like that
      unpredictable, heat
      a necessity, an evil
Then thought
      you wear red – well.

Just a Splash, Not Quite a Whole Cup, 1993

(Dee "We Be Nappy" Snell)

Just a splash, not quite a whole cup

Take it easy

Don't fill it up.

Just a splash is all I need for now anyway

That's about right

I'll get more another day.

Just a splash; I only want to taste it

That's quite enough

I don't want to waste it.

Just a splash

    of laughter at your story

   -of twinkle in your eye

   -of praise about His glory

   -of memories gone by just a splash

    of coffee after dinner

   -of wine in candlelight

   -of fame as a winner

   -of peace for doing right, just a splash

of being somebody's lover

-of the hope that comes also

-of settling for no other

-of watching each other grow.

Just a splash   of life today

I have until I die to fill it up!

Winking Women, 2001

Winking women
always makes me wonder
what you see inside of me
that you'd assume
I'd understand
why you winked at me
implying familial identity
or suggesting shared secrecy
but before I ask or even get your name
I impulsively wink back
and we both keep on walking by.

Just Because: Duet

(with Kimberly Redefining Freedom McCrae)

Just because I'm smiling doesn't mean there's nothing wrong.
It may mean I know the difference between the rhythm and the song.

Just because I'm dancing doesn't mean the music's fine.
It may be what's keeping me from losing my mind.

Clarity of purpose is the enemy of lack
Keeps the spirit thriving
Keeps the soul from turning back

There's nothing to go back to
None but darkness
None but lack

So I'll keep smiling
I'll keep dancing
While time keeps moving on

And we'll fight to make it better
By and by

Just because I'm writing doesn't mean I know my voice
It may mean I want to speak, but I feel devoid of choice

Just because I'm moving doesn't mean I'm on my way
It may mean my spirit's been oppressed, so I fear I cannot stay

Clarity of vision is the goal of those with sight
Those who have the confidence to speak into the night

Those with the spirit of Sojourner
Who will stand
For what is right
Ones who journey
Towards our freedom
Not relenting day by day

As we fight to make it better
By and by

Little Mannish Women, 2011

to all the little mannish women who aint scared of my thicker, fine 5'9"

Ya'll know who you are
You little mannish women

Who wears Stacey Adams in Mens 5.5
and learned to tie the Windsor Knot mirrorless

better than you ever did a bow ribbon on a pigtail in your prior life.

Whose dime-faced Lady Timex
morphed into the half-dollar-faced man-sized Bulova
with a two-inch wide distressed leather band – in brown.

Who aint scared of pastel argyles or mixing up underwearings
Victoria's Secret with Jocky's sports or
Joe's Boxer with 18 hour-cross-your-heart
when your girls need a little extra support.

Who situates the chapeau and bends the baseball just right
like a calling card in the halls of justice or a picket sign that never
fades
as you swag to move the center closer to our fringes.

Who stood in the 'charming smile' line at Creation
and wrote the book on 'How to Smile and
Get the Panties Without Even Trying – Hard'
Little mannish women – you!

You know who you are.
Feeling all your womanliness
Looking so-so-so mannish
to some, conflicted impossibility
to other, an ontological dichotomy
But you, you feel yourself and say
"Just Right!"
And I agree.

Little mannish women
got swagga in sweetness
as soft as you wanna be
hard when you gotta be

understands why wearing lingerie
and being strapped simultaneously
just makes good sense, and
hella, hella, hella good sex

knows how to fix a flat tire, but
calls Triple A, because
the mani/pedi is fresh

Little mannish women
I pay homage to your courage to
believe that my big womanly roundness is
for your touch to conquer and
to show my heart its way home.
Little mannish women
Ya'll know who you are.
Working me when all you did was
walk into the room.

Moonlight

When You See a Woman Dancing, 1995

When you see a woman dancing
especially if alone
Don't be too quick to become a partner
to help choreograph the song

just watch her dance
identify the clues
See the rhythm of her feet
 clothed in mourning shoes

She may just have to bend her knees,
sway and arch her back
To counter the day's oppression
or in preparation for attack

She may just have to lift her arms
in a woman's soulful way
Remembering now to love herself
after another long, hard day

She may just very well be praising
God or her God-given man
For treating her like a lady
and taking time to understand

So, when you see a woman dancing
don't be too quick to join her
instead, could you simply concur
That she is just dancing
for herself?

Tangents, 1995

Tangents
fell from my lips
when from my hips, I wanted to dance
'cause the music sounded soooo good
I was a'rocking and a'reeling
a'swinging and a'swaying
a'rocking and a'reeling
a'swinging and a'swaying
I was having

Tangents
flowing from hips
falling past my lips
spilled into my hands

Tangents
of caressing you
of making chocolate chip cookies

Tangents
of doing stuff that hands do
to make you feel good
to make him look good
to make me be good to myself

Tangents.

What My Poem Sounds Like, Moves Like, 2002

jazz hands

ohh ahh dadadatdat
ohh ahh dadadatdat

raise hands over head

flow Spirit to me
from my worship of You
all of me open to Your presence

bring hand down along left of body

come Spirit to me
to this processional for You
all of me open to Your presence

bring hands up along right of body

fill Spirit, fill me
right now right now will You
all of me open to Your power

raise hands over head

ohh ahh dadadatdat
ohh ahh dadadat dat

jazz hands

Instant Intimacy, 1995

Instant intimacy
quickly grows cold
like oatmeal from the microwave
Wouldn't you really rather boil my water
before you roll my oats?

Coffee, 1995

Five foot two or six foot four
it's a certain kind of man that I adore
like a good cup of coffee to get me on my feet
I like that man very seldom, very black, and very sweet!

Never needed it often; coffee that is
always want just one to claim me as his
never needed cream either, didn't like the fat
always wanted one that, through and through, was black.

With money rolls or just pocket change
basic flavor or exotic and strange
a good cup of coffee just can't be beat
if, like the man, it is very seldom, very black, and very sweet!

In My Mind's Eye, 1983

In my mind's eye
With visions of omnipotence
I see the world in view;

Overlooking eternity,
Oblivious of the distance
I see the love in you.

In my mind's eye
Searching eagerly
 for release, I seek a welcoming heart;

To be consumed by joy
To be showered with peace
I see you as a part of,

The total picture that I see In my mind's eye.

You Might As Well, 1994

You might as well
 write me into your history
'cause after a kiss like that
you'll never speak the same language of love again.

You might as well
reach out and touch someone coast to coast
command the locker room mic and boast.

You might as well
since I am now recorded in your head
and my perfume lingers in your bed.

You might as well.

Take a Deep Breath, 1995

Hey! I can breathe   again!

Been holding my breath
for a long five years
it is a wonder I didn't pass out or die
although I almost did –
or did I?

Naw!
 'Cause right now
 I can breathe   again!

A Needed Break, 1988

While you were away
I returned phone calls 3 weeks old
Did laundry and dusted 3 weeks' worth of both
Played 3 hours of video games
 at the club of 3 flavors
 (great score, enter our initials)
3 times with you in mind
Got 3 extra hours of sleep each night
but without fail
woke up at 3 each morning
3 hours early for waking for work
just to think of you
Read 3 chapters of 3 books I'd bought the day
we met 3 weeks ago
Needless to say,
I've gotten 3 layers deeper into you
(this is serious!)
and have shed 3 layers of protection
that defending wall which exists
between each our hearts to fend off
needed love and unneeded pain
Not that I don't miss you, mind you
it's just that I needed this week of you away
to touch base with reality

I'll welcome your return, knowing that
you needn't be away for me to
resume my life
but can add you to it
Pieceably

I Spent the Day Smelling for You, 1995
(LDG)

I spent the day smelling for you
seeking your scent, which caused sensations
 in my senses   all of them...

I sought at cologne counters
caressing custom cast bottles
claiming the essence of potions
contained therein   but none of them...

I opened each one for a whiff
wondering if it would be your
wonderful, warm way of wooing me
with each embrace   but not a one of them...

I spent the day smelling for you
all the time missing...
the processional to a hearty laugh by a gap-toothed smile
just enough stubble and sweat to delight my cheeks
strong hands skilled in caressing and construction
stronger mind able to preach, teach, and reach me
that which was   missing YOU!

Wake-up Call, 2002

carole m.

>   I waited
for your wake-up call
>   you said
you'd be gentle   and
>   I waited
for your gentleness
call, kiss, caress
>   you said
>   I'll come
>   I waited

I can't tell whether I woke up
early   on time   on my own
or whether I never really did sleep
much at all last night because
>   you said
>   I'll come
Wait a minute
let me fall asleep again.

Thots of You, 2002

thots of you
makes me wanna   touch myself

hold my own hand
finger my own palm
kiss inside my own wrists

breathe moist warmth on my own neck
entangle my locs to the roots
pull my head back and up into position to kiss

caress my own full breasts
trace voluptuous curves from my own waist
massage dull longing in the small of my back

tenderly spank my own firm butt
firmly part my own thick thighs
slowly stroke these long, lovely hirsute legs

thots of you   imagine this
makes me wanna   remember when
I touch myself   like you will when you finally
                          call me close enough to
                          touch me for yourself.

Lotta Words, 2002

I usually have a lotta words
 making my point
painting a picture
singing a song
dancing like crazy
teaching with heart
thinking out loud
reading with attitude

but you   walk into the room

and, alas,   I am speechless

I Would Come Out If, 2002

I would come out if
you would be my guide
navigating love   and hate
committing to stay beside me
when I doubt that I can do this
but never doubting that I can /do love you.

I would come out if
you would hold me close   in private
until I got the courage to hold your hand in public
to introduce you
and reintroduce me   without stuttering
to family   friend   other kin

I would come out if
when I need to sit and silently cry
(because that is what I do when I am afraid)
you do not wonder whether I am planning to flee
but that you know without a doubt
that through my tears, I am merely
watering this Garden   our love

I would come out if
you would help me
color outside the lines
create a pretty picture
we'd admire together
hang on loving display.

Coffee: the Remix, 2002

Five foot two or six foot four
it's certain kind of wm'yn that I adore
like a good cup of coffee to get me on my feet
I tend to like `em bold, black, and sweet!

Never needed it often   coffee, that is
always just wanted that one that was hard to resist
never needed cream either didn't like the fat
always just wanted one   through, and through is black!

With money rolls or just pocket change
basic flavor   exotic or strange
a good cup of coffee just can't be beat
if like the wm'yn it's bold, black, and sweet!

September Watermelon, 1997

Tastes so sweet
 refreshing cool
 Indian summer heat

lick my lips   suck my tongue
remember this sweetness
in August, you were the one

that cooled me down
from head to feet
with touch and taste
your nectar so sweet

but right now, its
September watermelon.

Succor, 2002

The way I turn my face towards you
 and you care enough not to look away
but allow me to gaze into your eyes
 not afraid you'd flee or criticize
expecting instead
that you'd do just what you do
 pull me closer into your bosom
 lay my head upon your breast
 hold me there just a little past a little while
 until my fear is gone
and my courage to love
and be loved by you
is restored.

Ear Candy, 2001

(FEW)

When you speak,   even when not to me
        speak that thang, speak that thang
Overheard in a crowd   quite accidentally
        speak that to me, speak that thang
I lick my lips at the very sound you see
        speak that thang, speak that thang, speak!
`Cause what is hear when you speak is   ear candy.

First overheard you talking to another across the room
Paying close attention   my heart began to swoon
As I leaned into listen   a distinctive G noted voice
My body began to tingle my ears did so rejoice!

When you speak   even when not to me
        speak that thang, speak that thang
Overheard in a crowd   quite accidentally
        speak that to me, speak that thang
I lick my lips at the very sound you see
        speak that thang, speak that thang, speak!
`Cause what is hear when you speak is   ear candy.

You were merely talking religion/politics to others still
As I edged a little closer my intrigue remained concealed
You slowed your pace dropped a key to clearly signify
My heart raced my face flushed this I can't deny!
The room is great the crowd so vast
I loose my nerve as you walk past

Grapes, Watermelon, & Women

How can I tell you that your voice is a feast
I remain unknown a foreigner among the least.

When you speak   even when not to me
        speak that thang, speak that thang
Overheard in a crowd   quite accidentally
        speak that to me, speak that thang
I lick my lips at the very thought you see
        speak that thang, speak that thang, speak!
`Cause what is hear when you speak is   ear candy.

You greet a friend, a honey dripping "hello"
Totally unaware just made my juices flow
And I'm yet not ready   for you to detect
My intrigue, ok, eavesdropping is so complex.

As you leave you share a laugh that makes me shudder
Risking a quick glance I begin to melt like butter
I quickly recover lest I would have to explain
Why I am falling all out and I don't even know your name!

When you speak   even when not to me
        speak that thang, speak that thang
Overheard in a crowd   quite accidentally
        speak that to me, speak that thang
I lick my lips at the very sound you see
        speak that thang, speak that thang, speak!
`Cause what is hear when you speak is   ear candy.

Fantasy Reprise:
Speak to me   speak to me   speak that thang to me!

Access, 1999

I was apprehensive
as I raised my top over my head
at your request
I was giving you access to my breasts
breast once swollen with nourishment for another's body
now smaller softer deflated globes of tenderness
sensitivity nonetheless
no longer cute and pert
now reminders of my womanhood
expressed though motherhood

Still you took time to give pleasure
where other lovers ignored.

Wet Curls, 1999

When your wet curls
wrap around my fingers
I linger feeling each fine strand
cupping the mass in my hand

physics would imply that
constant friction would dry
the moisture from your curls   my fingers
but I linger
and you drip drip   sigh   ooze
pleasure
as my fingers treasure
every wet curl.

Marked, 1999

You marked my skin with your teeth
with passion that would fade a day or two later
no sign a mark was made.

Still often it is instead that after the marks depart
I still can feel the ones you made
with your touch on my heart.

Phantom pain and pleasure
run the length of my spine
where your teeth had marked me
where you touch declared mine.

Some days I fear I'll never know again your teeth marks
on my skin but never does a day go by that
 I fail to feel your marks within.

Come, Again, 1999

The night was long and laborious
we'd bump grind moan and sigh

wait a minute
you want some water
I need some air
we laugh touch and smell
at our intermission
not intermittent
love making
I can't wait to come
are you sure that you will
do you doubt it
      breathe sensual
      taste sexual
      hear spiritual
      see sensible
I knew I would come   hummm
I was just waiting   hummm
for you to want   hummm
me to.   Ahhhh hummmmm
Come, again.

Hunger Pangs, 1997

I missed my nourishment today
That upon which I feast when you call to say
Good morning   as the new day is dawning.

I missed the daily bread of your voice
That reminds me every time
that we made the choice   to love
who each other brings.
I missed the filling of your touch
The way even across the miles in
which you convey much in your   Good night
that makes my day all right
I missed you.
And now,
I am hungry.
Oh,   so   hungry.

Too Busy, 1997

Yesterday, we got too busy and that aint good
Too busy to place a call
        Like a lover would.

Too busy to put on hold calls   from all over the place
That we could place a call
        Longing to see a lover's face.

Too busy to step away from demands all around
To reach out and touch the
        Sure thing we say we've found.

Yesterday we got too busy
Can we promise not to let it happen again?
Can we make this promise to ourselves?
As lovers   and as friends?

Eventuatin', 2001

(Carol)

Eventuatin' is waiting
for the best man to come along
or maybe even a woman's song
waiting
for this too to pass
good success to last
waiting
for children to grow up   and out
still a distant the empty nest shout
waiting
for stocks to turn
banking money to bum
waiting
for harvest bulbs to bloom
come spring   come soon
Eventuatin' is waiting
for warmth to feet so cold
come on now   get on over here
before I get too old
Eventuatin' is waiting
         in the meantime
         somebody
         pass me some socks.

Non Verbal, 1997

When you walk away
into the distance   conveyed in your voice
what should I think?
how shall I wait?
where ought I be?
when you return   on what date, again?

Lost My Heart, 1999

I looked amidst the tousled covers
bent face to the floor to
survey under the bed collection

I rifled through drawers of clean lingerie
just in case I'd folded and packed away

I unzipped all the pockets
on the three piece luggage
and ran my hands in every hidden fold

I flipped the mattress, sofa cushions and area rug
aware that it might have slipped into a crevice

I even sorted through stacks of mail, trash cans
and old magazines in case I absent mindedly
filed it away for safe keeping.

I'm exhausted from looking
and have come to realize that
I've done gone and lost my heart
to loving you   irretrievably.

DNA, 1997

I put off changing sheets and pillow cases
hand washing silks and delicate laces
dusting table tops and window sills
 tossing junk mail and make-a-deals.
for as long as I could
until you told me as a command
to wash up and put away
leave no proof that you had lay
 in my bed and in my arms
news to cause others alarm
and as I moved to put in place
all these things leaving no trace
that you have brought great smiles to my face
whew! Not a trace of DNA left in this place.
Are you always so thorough and complete
to pack up your belongings and command to wash the sheets

You took all you brought and wiped away finger prints
But still, dear one, the love scene holds much evidence.
And not all is circumstantial.
My smile is brighter,
My hips jiggle and switch
My laugh reverberates
You satisfied a longing itch.
Yeah, you might have cleared out your DNA
But consider yourself convicted, you left some D-A!

Poetry, 1999

I didn't write poetry
while you were here
'cause I had the chance   instead
to perform it live   upon our bed.

Companionship, 1999

Could we be
content with companionship
making covenant   without ceremony
to celebrate   cry   care appropriately
defined by what
is convenient cost efficient carefully closeted
could we be
content with companionship
choosing words
crafting responses
culling emotions
to keep safe   keep centered   keep sacred
could we be content with companionship
or
would we just be wasting
our wills   and wants   and work
on that which will never be?

Vanilla Candles, 1997

Candles burn in every room
filling each with sweet perfume
fragrance pungent fragrant mellow
still I cannot burn vanilla.

It's my favorite   you once said
As we lay upon my bed
with no intent to fall asleep
with passion taking us in too deep.

I tried to light it   once I did
but choose instead to replace the lid
for fear the slightest whiff would lead me
to long for you to want and need me.

Perhaps some day, just not tomorrow
I'll burn vanilla and not feel sorrow
but will instead follow its fragrant bliss
to the happiest memories
your breath
your touch
your kiss.

Silent Partners, 1997

Silent partners speak volumes
that only they can hear
 even though others strain to listen
 to what they are saying

when the slightest glance lingers
and when the gentlest touch burns
and when an inside joke is understood

by only the two of us
 because the two of us
became silent partners.

Naming, 1997

We fail as lovers or is it too soon to tell
 even though at your voice my tender places swell?

To say we're sisters falls somewhat short of the mark
although when being silly we share a sister's heart.
Friends usually work in a rather generic sense
except when a knowing one perceives where we've been.

Confidantes work, for a while anyway
as our minds remain open as we struggle with what to say.
Partner, now that's the epitome or so I imagine and yearn
more about what this means more of your heart I learn.

So there it is laid out and plain a multifaceted view
of desires and possibilities of how I see being with you.
But today as we journey and walk hand in hand
I can't see where we're going nor name it promise land.

Still one thing is certain, yes, of this one thing I am sure
I am here to walk with you with a love that will endure ... naming.

I'm Gonna Be Alright

After You Throw It Up, 1985

I remember too well the stench and
how everything felt porcelain white and
cold   because it was

and the pain   a dull throbbing pain
 that took turns with a knife sharp
reminder of the reasons
but there should be no reasons
not worth this kind of pain
I remember thinking

and it came so fast
but in a rhythm of its own
out of sync with my heartbeat
and it splattered on the wall the floor
more porcelain and cold   because it was

and the stench
and the pain
and the salted tears of mere frustration
and it's tomorrow that I'll think
at least when you throw it up
it ain't in you anymore.

Lonely: Played in the Key of G, 2002

Calling out to every ache and pain
Ever-present company
To each you''ve given name.

Mocking diagnoses of OCD
Creating even new ones
Constructin prisons, can imagine being free.

Taking pictures mentally, posed on video
Other people's joy
Where are what happened yours only memory of long ago?

Striking a nerve, a key to left of C
Lonliness, you say
Is your main problem,
play this song in the key of G.

Tomorrow, Next Week, and Never, 1983

I told you
"Look Baby, I have a wonderful night planned
a candle lit dinner complete
with violins and a '21 vintage
we can watch the sun set as we
cuddle in front of the big bay window
overlooking eternity and seduce each other
with eyes and gentleness.
How about it, Baby? Huh?"

And you told me
"Tomorrow."
(period)

I told you
"Honey, I won this raffle for a weekend for two
on the lake at Mt. Bonnell complete
with cabin and cablevision
We can watch the city below us
transform from a hustle
to a slow drag in pin lights
And, make love under the moon
in the middle of the night
 on the lake in the canoe.
How about it, Baby? Huh?"

And you told me
"Next week."
(period)

Tomorrow?
Next Week?

Well, to me Baby those words are
synonymous with Never.

So, I guess that I'll eat my dinner, alone
dance to my violins, alone
and get drunk on that '21 all by myself
`Cause my love was not laid on Never.

And, I'll cool out at the cabin, alone
play connect the dots with the lights below, alone
and let the moon move the waters
and rock me
all by myself
`Cause my life won't wait on Never.

I guess that I'll be seeing you around
say, like Tomorrow?
or maybe, Next Week?
And by the way, Baby,
don't forget in my vocabulary
Tomorrow and Next Week
are synonymous with Never!

The Morning After Peace, 1995

The morning after you left
I woke up and watched myself get back together

The first peace found was a good night's rest   not just sleep
not an ache in my body or heart   a smile upon them both

Then I found the peace of silence
the volume of ignoring me finally turned off
the murmer of your t.v. behind closed doors
no longer the insult to meals without you

Oops!
Almost tripped over a peace of dance
 held captive the past five years
but followed my feet to releve', plie
and my hands to snap, clap and sway

All through the day I found peaces of
breathing deeply, talking loud and laughing
of running errands because I needed
to not for escaping for an hour

The night after you left
I bathed a body more whole than it had been in a while
than which I could have been much longer

The morning after you left
I watched the pieces I'd become
become more of a full peace again.

I Got the Power to Heal, 1995

I got the power to heal
not by forgetting you
but by remembering me

remembering who I was
before I became your puppet and pawn
before I wept all night and
before I dreaded the dawn

I got the power to heal
by remembering me
before you.

Secrets, 1995

Not telling
made it easy for you to lie
for me to die
for us to hide our fear and shame
regrets of our common name
realities of mutual blame

Not telling
made it easy for you to deceive
for me to grieve
for you to leave me
and the son we had
leaving no time for me to be sad
realizing this is not at all so bad

Not telling made it easy.

The Sleeper's Nightmare, 1996

When both of us are not dreaming
 it becomes the sleeper's nightmare
 and so I can no longer be the
keeper of the pieces of the dream
because I woke up and realized
I'd been lulled into the
billowy clouds of superficiality
the darkness of an abusive reality
and that you were awake
and aware the whole time.

When both of us are not dreaming
it becomes the sleeper's nightmare

Darkness, 1987

Long after you are asleep I lay awake
listening to the sounds of the Universe
stars watching clandestine lovers l
ike telling eyes they are
moons lighting the paths back home,
to here, or somewhere else
and the Darkness shielding me
from knowing and being known
comforting me from feeling and being felt
and I wait breathlessly for dawn.

Long after you are asleep I lay awake
feeling the life in this house
walls speaking of passion and pain
the adage made real to me
if these walls could talk
stairs bearing footsteps of our
coming, going, having company
and the Darkness
hiding my silent tears
that show only on my face

and are felt deep from my soul
cleansing me of today's pain of being here
where I'm least wanted and most needed
but not feeling like anything
 but Darkness.
Long after you are asleep
I lay awake.

The Bottom of My Tears, 1995

At the bottom of the lake
is where they almost found me
'cause I found a worm first
at the bottom of the tequila and
headed to rock bottom
over trying to jump through hoops
 that just kept getting higher
and I kept ending up on the bottom
Thank God (and I mean, really, stop and do it)
 the last time I looked up and saw the bottom
I laughed at my own pitiful self
I laughed so hard
I laughed so long
I laughed so deep

I cried
For the last time on the bottom
I cried
And I found laughter at the bottom
of my tears.

Scars, 2002

I spent a lot of time and inconvenience

     Summer time in long sleeves

     Pool time is biker shorts

     Night time with the lights out

     Bath time in a hush and a hurry.

I spent a lot of time and inconvenience

     Hiding all of my scars.

When I really wanted you to kiss them

     But would simply die if you saw them

Longed for you to caress the tell-tale signs that

     I had been hurt but that you with me here

       is my healing.

A Change in the Weather, 2001

Winter took ahold of my heart
way before summer ended
and I've been sitting by this here fire
trying to thaw it, darn it, mend it.

I rocked it like a baby
'cause I just wouldn't stop crying
hardened from the core to the edges
'cause of all your years of lying.

I wrapped it up in blankets
of soulful tunes on the radio
massaged it daily with pungent oils
but that stubborn old hurt refused to go.

Laid it, unattended
on the hearth for a while
touched it every now and then
seeking a forgotten smile.

[unfinished poem]

My Empty House is Full, 1997

I walk around my empty house   smiling
emptied of fear and restless nights
emptied of fighting or choosing flight
emptied of longing for intimacy

and now, my emptied house
 is filling up with love!

Proof Poem, 1995

You boldly mocked my confidence
 found the day   I finally left you

even though you left me   two years before
to return to your mama's house
to make a way and find a house
to call my own for our son

even though you left me
just before
Thanksgiving   Christmas
Kwaanza   New Years
                          and Valentine's Day
and knowing that   just for you I
cooked turkey   didn't bake fruit cake
didn't put bell peppers in the black eyed peas
hand cleaned 20 pounds of chittlins
and waited all day for a special delivery
just for you

You boldly mocked my confidence found
the day I finally left you.

Today   I finally   left you
and this poem is my proof.

Not Gonna Wake Up Soon, 1996

you are not supposed to fit
into my daydreams   night fantasies
but you move   in and out of them
staying longer   and longer and longer
causing me to hope that out from them
you come closer   and closer   and closer.